Dr. Seuss' HOW THE GRINCH STOLE CHRISTMAS!

Grinch & Bear It!

Life According to the Supreme Green Meanie!

Based on the
motion picture screenplay by
Jeffrey Price & Peter S. Seaman

Based on the book by Dr. Seuss

RANDOM HOUSE 🏠 NEW YORK

"The term *Grinchy* will apply
when Christmas spirit is in short supply."
—*The Book of Who*

Sometime in the years after the publication of Dr. Seuss' classic *How the Grinch Stole Christmas!*, the word *grinch* entered our language as a term meaning "a person or thing that spoils or dampens the pleasure of others." (It's in Webster's— you can look it up!) In other words, it describes someone who indulges in stingy, "bah, humbug type" behavior, just as the Grinch did when he stole Christmas from the citizens of Whoville.

When Theodor Geisel—better known as Dr. Seuss—wrote his best-selling book in 1957, he meant it as a cautionary message to all of us. He was saying that we were losing sight of the true meaning of

Christmas. The holiday, which had begun as a joyous religious celebration, was becoming hopelessly buried under an onslaught of crass commercialization. The joyous themes of Christmas past had become—as personified by the Whos' pre-holiday frenzy—buy, buy, buy and spend, spend, spend.

How the Grinch Stole Christmas! shows us, through Cindy Lou Who's innocent faith and the Grinch's transformation, that we mustn't forget the true meaning and spirit of Christmas as a time for giving—of ourselves and our love—to others.

Dr. Seuss' *How the Grinch Stole Christmas!* is a magical story that has been transformed into a brilliant comic movie with heart and with a universal message about goodness and generosity at a time when such a message is needed more sorely than ever.

Here's to the true spirit of Christmas!

—*The Editors*

ON BEING A WHO

No matter how different
a Who may appear,
he'll always be welcomed
with Holiday Cheer.

—*The Book of Who*

Every size of Who
we can measure
knows that Whobilation
is a time we must treasure.

—*The Book of Who*

The Cheermeister is one who deserves
a cheer, a backslap, or a toast!
It goes to the soul at Christmas
who needs it most.
—*The Book of Who*

Since Christmas cards are sent by mail
the Postal Service must never fail.
—*The Book of Who*

ON THE WHO-LETIDE

We've got to keep shop-shop-shopping!
— *Lou Lou Who*

That's what it's always been about,
isn't it? Gifts! Gifts! Gifts! Well, let me
tell you what happens to your gifts:
They all end up coming to me...
in your garbage...at the dump!
— *The Grinch to the assembled Whos*

This is my favorite day of the year:
three days before Christmas!...
Then, of course, there's two days
before Christmas—and Christmas Eve...
Then again, there's Christmas itself...
Then again, there's the day *after* Christmas!
You know what? They're all great!

—*Lou Lou Who*

Now let's just concentrate on having the best
Christmas ever!

—*Mayor May Who*

ON THE WHOBILATION

I tell you people *one* thing:
Invite the Grinch, destroy Christmas.
But did anyone listen?

—*Mayor May Who*

I just wanted everyone to be together for Christmas.

—*Cindy Lou Who*

Who knows? This Whobilation could change my entire outlook on life.

—*The Grinch*

Well…if you Lou Whos have finished desecrating the most important day of the year, maybe now we can all get back to Christmas the way it should be—Grinchless.

—*Mayor May Who*

They'll bang on ting-tinglers and blow their floo-flounders; they'll bash their jing-jinglers and bounce on boing-bounders.

—*The Grinch*

Nutcracker! It's their Whobilation! I can't watch another minute of this.

—*The Grinch*

TO HIS FAITHFUL DOG, MAX

Fleas before beauty.

—*The Grinch*

Hello, Max. Are you having a holly jolly Christmas?

—*The Grinch*

All right! You're a reindeer. Here's your motivation: You're Rudolph, you're different, you can't play any reindeer games. Then Santa picks you and you save Christmas—wait, no you don't, forget that part. We'll improvise. You *hate* Christmas; you're going to steal it. Saving Christmas was a lousy ending, totally unrealistic. And...Action!

—*The Grinch*

I don't know why you're laughing, Rudolph…
—*The Grinch*

Work it, Max. Feel the burn. All you!
—*The Grinch*

ON HEARTS

Look, it's the size of a baby pea!
>—*The Grinch on the state of his heart*

O bleeding hearts of the world unite!
>—*The Grinch*

Oh, no, Max,
help me!
I'm…
FEELING!
>—*The Grinch*

What's happened to me? I'm all toasty inside.
Oh, Max...I love you.

—*The Grinch*

We knew
right away
he was…special.
—*Clarinella*

He was a
wonderful little…
whatever-he-was…
—*Clarinella*

My, haven't
you turned
out to be
a handsome,
odd-looking
whatever-
you-are!
—*Clarinella*

[The Grinch] is a what who just doesn't like Christmas.

—*Lou Lou Who*

Santa?
Don't forget
the Grinch.
I know he's
mean and hairy
and smelly.
His hands
may be cold
and clammy.
But I think
he's actually
kinda…sweet.

—*Cindy Lou*

ON BEING A GRINCH

I've got to do something.
Those Whos have to pay.

—*The Grinch*

How dare you enter the Grinch's lair?!?
You little micro-menace! The impudence!
The audacity! The unmitigated gall! You will
rue the day you came here! You called down
the thunder; now get ready for the Boom.
Gaze into the face of fear!!!!!

—*The Grinch to Cindy Lou*

All right, Whoville, if you're hungry for
humbug, I'm the special of the day!...
and I deliver!

—*The Grinch*

ON BEING GRINCHY

Four Whos, one Grinch. I'll take those odds…
—*The Grinch*

Serves them right,
those yuletide-loving,
sickly sweet,
nog-sucking
cheermongers.
I mean, I really
don't like 'em.
Mm-mm, no,
I don't.
—*The Grinch*

Fat Boy should
be finishing up any
time now. Talk about
a recluse. He only comes
out once a year—you don't see him catching
any flak…

—*The Grinch*

Ya got me, Officer. I did it. I am the Grinch who stole Christmas and I'm sorry. Don't you want to cuff me? Put me in a choke hold. How about pepper spray? I deserve it. I'm a loose cannon. I'm a live wire. I'm a threat to society!

—*The Grinch*

GRINCH-ISMS

Be it ever so heinous,
   there's no place like home.
                    —*The Grinch*

Right...
  See, the North Pole's
  being renovated.
 So I'm working out of
 the South Pole this year.
Got a little time-share with
the Tooth Fairy and, you know,
Sasquatch. Good guy. I gotta go.
                    —*The Grinch*

And now for the final brushstroke
 of my stinky rotten masterpiece
 of...not-niceness!
 Oh, the wailing
 and the gnashing of teeth!
 It'll be music to my ears!
                    —*The Grinch*

Nothing like a little snowball fight
to break the ice.

—*The Grinch*

You see, Max, one man's compost heap is
another man's potpourri.

—*The Grinch*

ON THE TRUE MEANING OF CHRISTMAS

Christmas is about being together with
our families and loved ones. And that's all.
Everything else is...superfluous.
And that means *unnecessary*.

—*Lou Lou Who*

I don't need
presents.
What more
could I want for
Christmas than
this?
  —*Lou Lou Who*

Because that's
not what
Christmas is
really all about,
gifts and contests
and fancy
lights...
  —*Lou Lou Who*

Welcome Christmas…
Christmas Day is in our grasp…
As long as we have hands to clasp…
—*The Whos*

Merry Christmas, Betty Lou. I have
absolutely nothing more to give you.
—*Lou Lou Who*

MERRY CHRISTMAS, MR. GRINCH!

I came to see you. No one should be alone
on Christmas.

—*Cindy Lou Who to the Grinch*

Merry Christmas, Cindy Lou!

—*The Grinch*